NOW
IS
THE HOUR

NOW
IS
THE HOUR

Native American Prophecies
and Guidance for the Earth Changes

ELISABETH DIETZ & SHIRLEY JONAS

with kindest regards from - Lisa Dietz

Blessings! Shirley Jonas

BLUE DOLPHIN PUBLISHING

Published by
Blue Dolphin Publishing, Inc.
P.O. Box 8, Nevada City, CA 95959
Orders: 1-800-643-0765

ISBN: 1-57733-029-3

LCCN:

Cover art by Wabimeguil (Betty Albert-Lincez)
Cover layout: Lito Castro

Printed in the United States of America

10   9   8   7   6   5   4   3   2   1

Dedication

*To the Seventh Generation
because our teaching is that everything we do
should be done so that we leave a better world
as far into the future as possible—
for the Seventh Generation.*

Elisabeth Dietz

Contents

Acknowledgments

The authors respectfully give thanks for permission granted to quote from the following elders:

Thomas Banyacya—Hopi
(c) 1990 Steve Wall and Harvey Arden
From the book *Wisdomkeepers* (Page 95)
Beyond Words Publishing, Inc., 1-800-284-9673

Leon Shenandoah—
Six Nations Iroquois Confederacy
(c) 1990 Steve Wall and Harvey Arden
From the book *Wisdomkeepers* (Page 105-106)
Beyond Words Publishing, Inc., 1-800-284-9673

and from *Dr. Pitcairn's Complete Guide to Natural Health For Dogs & Cats* © 1995 by Richard H. Pitcairn and Susan H. Pitcairn. Permission granted by Rodale Press, Inc., Emmaus, PA 18098. For ordering information: 1-800-848-4735

They also give heartfelt thanks to their helpmate, Shirley's sister, Frances Turney. Without her understanding and belief in the message and the hours she spent typing, this book would have taken many more weeks to put together.

Lisa's Message

Prophecies and Prayerful Guidance

We await the dawn of a new day
A new age full of hope for all.
I pray for all of us.
I pray for my children and yours.

From the ORAIBI HOPI NATION

Arizona, April 1993

Counting on his fingers, a Hopi elder stood and spoke, "You have been telling the people that this is the eleventh hour. Now, go and tell them:

THIS IS THE HOUR!

"There are ten things to consider—
Where are you living?
What are you doing?
What are your relationships?
Are you in the right relationships?
Where is your water?
Know your garden.
It is time to speak your truth.
Create your community.
Be good to each other.
Do not look outside yourself for the leader."

Then he brought his hands together in a clasp and said, "This could be a Good Time."

I speak to you from my place of paradise, my piece of Turtle Island that we call Mother Earth, the southern shores of Lake Superior in the Upper Peninsula of Michigan.

In the winter the snow covers the dark pines with grace and beauty and the fresh water icebergs, forty to fifty feet high, crash and crunch the shorelines. In the spring and summer these tremendous waves, during an occasional storm, bring up treasure from the depths of this beautiful lake and sprinkle the broad white sand beaches with all kinds of mysterious things.

I camp where a creek meanders out into the lake dividing itself among silver sandbars, like a tongue of green, splashed here and there with colors of pink, white, green, yellow and red and, until you look closer, you cannot distinguish whether these are strawberries, flowers or butterflies.

Here is my little summer tent in a place where my Grandmother always put her tent to pick blueberries and to do the fasting that is required by the women of the Anishabe Nation (the first people) in Spring and Fall.

I feel, as I stand looking out at the water, with the sun in my face and the wind lifting my hair, that all these women, my ancestors are inside me, like so many layers of an onion that have finally produced who I am today. I feel the medicine women, the good mothers, the strong women, the shy quiet women of our people all standing within my skin.

I feel the memories within the racial subconscious and I also feel, because these women are me and further generations will also be me, I can, with a little projection, tune into the past or the future. I believe that this is where the gift of second sight comes to us as a people. The ability to go back and forth between the seen world and the unseen world.

When I was a child I had visions that people would regard as nightmares, from as early as I can remember. I had good dreams, too, but had no clue as to what these dreams and visions meant. Then as I grew older I began to see places and things that would jar the memories of the dreams and visions from childhood. I began to trust the fact that the dreams and visions were in fact telling me stories and those stories became today's news and then became history. So I have to think that the visions that I had as a young child, as well as the ones over a half century of life . . . that these things are tomorrow's history. If this is true (and I know that this is so) then it is a great responsibility.

What I speak of here is only my truth, seasoned by the traditions and beliefs of my culture.

In my travels I have contacted a network of many of our elders. They have told me things that I need to pass on to all people who are meant to hear.

Messages and Teachings from the Elders

I sit on the high banks of sand dunes and rock, with the sweet grass and wild flowers all around me. These things are a feast to my eyes, my heart and spirit. I think about this beautiful place and the world, my piece of Turtle Island, if things are allowed to go on as they are. We can't allow all that is wondrous, this paradise, to be destroyed in the name of progress . Progress is for our souls, not for the material things that we think we need. I feel that the Creator will not allow this.

The elders have told me that many years ago there were those among us who woke up in a cold sweat in the middle of the night and called for their people to come to their tepees and wigwams to hear the terrible things that they had seen. They had seen death and destruction, not just for us, but for our land, our animals, our air and our water. Tears were shed by some of these traditional people. Tears that were so strong that they were almost the consistency of blood. Some of our people thought that this could never be. But because it was our way to believe our visionaries, to have respect for our traditional people, most believed that this is the way it would be.

I thought about what had been said so long ago, as I watched the seagulls ride the air currents in the bright blue sky over the water and looked at the white sand in my hand sprinkling like diamonds through my fingers. I heard the echo of these prophecies within my soul and my mind and my heart ached. I went within and listened to the words of my ancestors reaffirming my dreams and my visions.

Many of the elders say that it is not right to share this knowledge with anyone who is non-native. I say, because of all that has gone on before, we don't know who is native and who is non-native because many of our Great Grandparents hid their heritage from their families in order to survive. So, when we look someone in the face, sometimes we are looking at one of our own. Perhaps, because reincarnation is part of our belief, then that "non-native" person sitting across from you may have been an ancient chief or medicine person. These things are kept in the heart of our Creator and we don't know. And because we don't know, we cannot judge.

Also, we have to understand that there are other universes out there with many other civilizations. Should this earth itself ever be attacked from without this globe, then we would all have to stand up as one and fight for our Turtle Island. If we were so threatened, then we would all be brothers. If we could be brothers and sisters under those circumstances, we must in fact be that now!

We are all the Creator's children for we have the same Father or Creator in common. For this reason, we often end our prayers by saying, ". . . all our relatives."

I am sure that, if these words were put out for society to read or to listen to, they would go unheeded by those who do not believe. Yet if they are needed by others, then I cannot deny them the ability to find and hear the truth.

At one time there were forty million of the "first people" Native Americans. Now there are maybe two million in North America. Many of us do not have the financial means to travel to that mountain top, or to that desert to find an elder that would teach them. So I will share what the Creator gave me and the Elders gave me with any of my children, with any of my Anishnabe sisters and brothers, with any other native person who needs to hear these messages, and will also not exclude *anyone* from my table if they are hungry for knowledge.

The normal way, the sacred way of expending teachings or information to each other is by oral tradition. This is the way of our people. Not on a computer or locked in a book. I am speaking this information from my mind's eye. I am in my cabin surrounded by tall cedar trees, with the sun falling gently all around. Sweetgrass hangs on the walls with sage burning and my cookstove crackling away making everything cheery.

I see generations to come who would not hear me if I were to share this only one on one. I see those who do not have the chance they need to come here to this spiritual place to listen to what I have to share. And I want to share these spoken words with as many as possible.

I am not "writing" this book. My friend who is my spirit sister is writing down my words as I speak. I am talking to you in the oral tradition of my people. My heart and my soul comes through these words. My only regret is that this oral testimony will go onto paper and you won't be able to hear the love that I have in my heart for all of you. All of you that are here now and all of you that are to come. I need to share this information because time is growing short and you don't have the time to seek out those of us who know.

When the brain hears spoken words, the learning takes place in a different part of the brain than that which is activated by reading. That may be why it is easier for us to remember what we learn from our oral teachings.

Often I've thought that who we learn something from is almost as important as what we learn.

I have come back to my home in the Upper Peninsula after a long journey, after many years of struggle for our spiritual rights, fishing rights, the rights of our children and the rights of our elders. I have spent many years asking my spirit guides to clear my mind, telling my body to "be quiet and leave me alone" so that my spirit could soar to places and see the signs. I have spent many days, weeks, and months sitting with my pipe offering tobacco, waiting for things to get better and seeing them get worse and knowing the price that was to be paid if we were foolish.

I have to acknowledge here the role of the pipes and that the pipes have come back and they have helped us. Because a lot of times the power of that pipe is such a strange power. A pipe that has a true spirit and is working well and treated well by its owner, it shows you many things and gives you that even when it is laying quietly and disassembled in its little leather bag. It still works for you. It still helps you. I acknowledge all the pipes and the pipe carriers who will take us through these difficult times to come.

People speak of the final conflict called "Armageddon." But they are all waiting for a physical war. This isn't how it is. The final conflict is just like the first one: it is going on, has been for ten years or more, *right now*. It is being fought in the unseen world. Forces for good and evil battle there. It is reflected in the seen world by all the violence. Many spiritual elders have fallen into the dark side. Many pipe-carriers have put away those pipes. I guess they got too heavy to carry. But this is exactly the time we should hold on to them and be praying!

Turtle Island, The Medicine Wheel, and the Mystery of the Land Bridge

*B*efore I tell you of my visions and of the prophecies, I need to give you the background of why we call this Turtle Island, the mysteries of the medicine wheel and the true facts of the land bridge, for all of this fits in and helps you understand the future and what we must do. I am speaking of the history of the Anishnabe and from what the old tradition has taught me as an Anishnabe or as a Chippewa person.

I acknowledge teachings I have received from elders of many other tribes including Hopi, Mayan, Menominee, Lakota. Most of their stories run about the same. We see these as stories because this is the way that our teaching goes. We sit down and we listen to what we are taught. It's a "story" in our culture, but we take it as absolute truth. Outsiders call it legend. It is not anymore strange for us to believe our truths than it is for us to look at your stories as truth in your Christian Bible, such as Moses parting the Red Sea and all the other things.

Millions of years ago Turtle Island was where we all lived. It was called Turtle Island because if you looked at the earth at that time all you saw was water except for a huge green round spot that looked like a giant turtle. The turtle's shell was made of many plates.

After a while these plates began to drift apart and as they drifted they formed different continents. Life formed on Turtle Island before the drifting started ... all non-human and animal. Spirits from the stars (the Sky People, or angels, if you will) danced in the air over this green island and watched the animals and birds and all of the Creator's creatures and wanted to become part of this creation and this beautiful island. The Creator took pity on these spirits and improved their shape so they could develop, have souls and journeys in the flesh to evolve into higher beings.

So the People drifted with the continents and formed communities in every part of the world, going in four different directions.

One of the most important teachings that we had in common was the Medicine Wheel. The four directions of the wheel represent earth, air, wind, and fire. We learned the four colors of man from this wheel and each division or color was responsible for one of the directions. The red race had the stewardship of the Earth and this is why we are speaking now. This is why we are trying to get our message across. We are the stewards of this earth, this part of Turtle Island that we live on here in North America.

The earth itself is in danger. The Mother Earth is being killed by her own children and this is a bad thing. And so we have this warning that, if things do not improve and if we don't stop cutting the forests, poisoning our water, our air and ourselves as well as our offspring, we'll end up exactly where we were in eons past when people had to flee, because the earth will tilt, shake, shudder and move again. This has happened in some degree or another three, maybe four, times. Proof of the earth having the great flood of 10,000 years ago is in our legends of the flood and in the Old Testament. This cycle occurs every 10,000 years or so, and therefore is now due.

North (white) Sweetgrass
The elders. The last part of
life. The white race who
have to learn the stewardship or manage fire in a
sacred way (judging from
the A-bomb, a long way to
go).

East (yellow) Tobacco
Represents the sunrise,
new life, spring. The
hope of the beginning or
renewal of life. Our
children. The yellow race
who have stewardship of
the air (Chi).

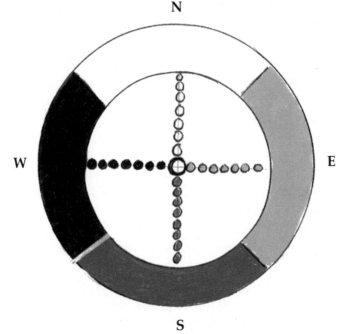

West (black or dark blue)
Sage
Represents the western door
we go through at the end of
our life, the third part of our
life also, and the black race
who have stewardship of the
water.

South (red) Cedar
Represents youth to mid-
age, summer, mid-day.
Raising our families. The
red race who have stewardship of the earth, who
know the earth does not
need or belong to us but *we*
need and belong to the
earth.

The yellow race, we learned, was responsible for the air. The black race was responsible for the water and the white race was responsible for the fire. How each race used these things determined their racial Karma. This is why the great Creator made each of the four races different. And we carry in our genes the subconscious memory of our responsibilities. Those of us with mixed blood are responsible for more than one of these directions. The Karma for North America is much greater than it is anywhere else for all four directions are now here! Our great land is a mixture of all these races. So we will have to answer for all of these, the fire the earth, the water and the air. All of that group Karma comes on the heads of us all . . . all of us who live on this piece of Turtle Island.

The scientific community has said that we migrated over a "land bridge" in the Bering Sea from Asia. We do not believe that this is so. The earth has shifted many times. A great wall of ice moving did not create a land bridge. On the contrary, it made a barrier or wall that kept us even more isolated. So, every time a shift occurred, rather than providing a bridge for people to migrate, it prevented them from coming here! Many of our elders think that this idea is so ludicrous that they won't even discuss it! They can't imagine why scientists would think that people who were such wonderful hunters would come thousands of miles over the ice, where there would be no game to live on during the journey, just to populate this area. We as a people have *always* been here! We were the first people here. We are the aborigines of this land. We came when our part of Turtle Island shifted and moved to make this great continent. We live here with the permission of the Great Spirit.

The blood type of most full bloods in the northern states is O positive, not A, AB, or B, as Asian ancestry would indicate. And the oldest archeological evidence of our being here is found as far south as Chile (South America) and predates the ice age.

Why Prophecy?
What We Traditional People Believe

*L*et me tell you now what some traditional Native Americans believe as far as prophecy is concerned. First, we believe that we live in the *now*. We don't need calendars as non-natives do. We go by the moon, the sun and the stars and the changing of the seasons. Our view of time is different. While you are using a calendar we live in what is called the "Eternal Now". What is happening now is what is important because you can't change what has happened in the past because it is already done. And you are not in the future yet. All you have is the NOW.

Mother Earth has an aura, a flow, a spirit. It is the work of an intelligent Being that designed everything to be the way it is. When we sleep within its body in that 'final' rest, we sleep within its soul and that soul nurtures us and feeds back into the very food that we eat from this earth, the very air that gives us our lives. We Native Americans understand the symbiotic relationship, the spirituality between ourselves and Mother Earth, and it keeps us always in tune.

People have injured our Turtle Island almost beyond the point of no return and we are to reap the rewards for our indifference. Mother Earth is angry for we have injured the soul that was left in our keeping and this soul will fight back to repair its aura in some terrible ways.

We have been told of the earthquakes which are happening now in increasing intensity all over the world.

These earth movements are the agony of our earth, the agony of its spirit, the fury of its pain.

We have much to endure to see our way through the devastation that is to come into our lives.

First, we must prepare our children for they are our future. They will carry the memories and we are to teach them to again become human beings. We have not done this. Instead, we have allowed the television to raise our children. The first five years they are raised by cartoon shows, the little Barney Dinosaurs, the little puppies and often violent cartoon animals. When they are big enough they are put on computer games and the children interact with that machine.

There is much danger in these videos and television. The danger is of thought plus energy equals reality . . . not just for our children but for millions of people in Alpha-state reinforcing the images that are projected before them on the screen. This violence on TV is creating violence! Those in Alpha watching violent movies will project these images into the ether by the millions. So done, the images will become fact.

Children don't understand patience, logic or structure because the calculator gives them rapid results. All "thinking" takes place outside their minds inside the computer.

We must wean our children from this. This is not how to teach our children to be human beings! When this child becomes a young adult he lacks compassion and doesn't know what it is to be caring. We wonder why we are having problems with our children! We have raised a whole generation of unemotional robots. When they marry and have children they won't be able to relate to their own children.

This is something we elders say has to change.

Technology has become our worst enemy. Technology has divided us from our rightful relationships. Even the stars have in this way been denied their rightful place in our lives. We live upon the Mother Earth and under the stars and we have been taught to forget. The robbing from our native culture of our knowledge of the Sun, Moon and Stars by the Judeo-Christian conquerors was one of the many wrongs done to us.

We are all part of cycles and these cycles occur with or without our belief in them. We still know the cycles of the seasons, the earth's droughts and floods, et cetera. But we must realize this all works together with cycles of the stars, moon and sun as well. Even a comet is a cycle, the most current one is a warning known as the Blue Star.

If the Mother, our earth, is sick, would not our Father the Sun get upset? With increased sunspot activity? Of course! So, you can expect not only the earth to be reacting, but the sun, too.

The sun is our life source. No seed can grow in Mother Earth without the Sun. But in coming times the Sun may be an angry Father that we misbehaving children must hide from. The Sun's future temper tantrums (solar flares) may pull the plug on the newest false idols: electricity and computer technology.

The Star People, Guardians, and Watchers

There are old stories of the Star People, the Guardians, the Watchers. I knew medicine men who sat with them in the circle to talk of things. It made no difference to these old ones if their guests came from Orion or Seattle as long as their talk was straight.

"No Eyes" told Mary Summer Rain that these watchers had withdrawn their protection. This is something that I also saw during a four day fast on Thunder Mountain in the spring of 1996. These "Watchers" might also be called guardian angels or Spirit Guides for the planet itself. But unique to some of them is that they guard the *air* of Mother Earth and some the earth's surface. They are tired of protecting us from our own carelessness and stupidity. Thus I saw them all sadly retreating and learned that the incidents of train, boat, and traffic accidents would increase. This would lead (hopefully) to raising the world's consciousness to make us more aware of our vulnerability and more compassionate toward our fellow man.

The increase of disasters in travel would also make us aware of our own mortality—to heighten our spiritual antenna to the trend of things to come; the changes we now cannot avoid. The withdrawal of protection heralds the inevitable. It should inspire us to prayer.

The Guardian Spirits of the air (usually referred to by Native Americans as the Four Directions, among other names) are also not protecting air travel anymore because we have so greatly abused the knowledge of using the air for travel. One of the single most destructive man-made contributions to the deterioration of the ozone layer is the incessant traffic of jet planes. Jet after jet takes off every second, some with only a handful of passengers. These jets suck in a great volume of our beautiful oxygen, burn it up and expel it as poisonous gasses. Hour after hour, day after day. This is destroying our air.

The Seven Campfire Prophecies and the Three Days of Darkness

*T*here have been many prophecies concerning the coming changes but our prophecies have a sense of direction. They have timing. They give signs.

The teachings of the Seven Campfires came to us over a thousand years ago.

At that time we all lived on the East Coast in peace and prosperity. Seven prophets came among our people, insisting that we must leave the coast of the Atlantic and move up the St. Laurence to safety inland, where we all now are. We were to travel until we came to the place where food grows on water (wild rice). If we stayed, they said, we would all die. Those few who disbelieved and stayed were wiped out.

To move several thousand people was quite a chore! But they did move.

Each campfire foretold what was to happen: The coming of the white man. The destruction of our people. The suppression of our spiritual ways. All of this came true. Our land was taken from us, our children lost their teachings and their dignity by being placed in white man's schools against their will. We were trampled into submission. All of this has happened and we are now in the time of the Seventh Campfire.

The seventh prophet said a New People would emerge to pick up what had been lost along the red road. (Because there are so many mixed bloods and half-breeds, we probably do look like a "new people.") And we have indeed rushed back to retrieve what was lost. All over now, sweat lodges, drum societies, and pipes are blossoming.

An Ojibway matron and elder from down the north shore said her aged uncle had told her, when you see sweat-lodges in everyone's backyards, the time (of purification) is very near. And today most of us have lodges in our backyards!

The seventh campfire was lit by a prophet who was young. It is thought that more young people than old will be followers of our ways by then.

It is with this campfire that we must watch which road our white brother takes. If they take the right and good road of enlightenment and return to spirituality, ecology, and balance, we would all live in peace and plenty.

But if he chooses to continue plundering the earth, burning thousands of years worth of fossil fuel in just one year without thought for the future generations, all will be lost. Their accumulated karma will backlash upon them.

Remember that all of the prophecies from these seven campfires were made a century ago. The six campfires have all come to pass, and we are now in the midst of that last one.

And this is where *we all* will decide our fate. "God" isn't punishing us. The sun isn't hurting us. (If we had not depleted the ozone and wounded Mother Earth, we would be given protection and shelter from the rays.) *We* have created our own past. That past is creating our future. *NOW* is when we must begin to act with common sense and spiritual awareness or face what we have done to ourselves. We must walk on this Earth in a Sacred Manner.

Chief Seattle said this so eloquently:

Teach your children
what we have taught our children—
that the earth is our mother.
Whatever befalls our earth
befalls the sons and daughters of the earth.
If man spit upon the ground
they spit upon themselves.
This we know
The earth does not belong to us,
we belong to the earth.
This we know
All things are connected
like the blood that unites one family
All things are connected.
Whatever befalls the earth
befalls the sons and daughters of the earth
We did not weave the web of life,
We are merely a strand in it.
Whatever we do to the web
We do to ourselves.

—Chief Seattle

There have been many visions of what Mother Earth looks like now. North America appears as a woman sleeping. Her hair is up in the Aleutian Islands and her body stretches all the way to South America. She is now throwing herself like a woman in fever, causing earthquakes. Her tears are becoming floods. The volcanic eruptions on her face are from toxic wastes that have been buried in Mother Earth. Soon she will become so ill that she will start pulling at her garments and then the earth will rip and these become more earthquakes and volcanic eruptions. She will toss and turn and our earth will tip and our earth will change as we know it.

Floods and erratic weather will become the order of the day. Once this happens, she will be in a "coma" and not hear us when we finally say, "Mother, we are sorry."

Our elders have told us the eruptions of the chemical and biological germs that are buried, especially in the west, will spread across our nation. These toxic waste dumps will burst forth into our atmosphere and, with volcanic ash, will become part of the three days of darkness that have been prophesied.

The three days will begin with violent earthquakes and volcanic eruptions. The clouds from the volcanos will become gigantic windstorms carrying the chemicals and the gases all across the world. The churning clouds will move like a living wall of dead air and carry the colors of four directions—white in the form of lightening, black in the form of blotting out the sun, red from the glow of the fire within and yellow from the poisons.

When that cloud comes, be prepared inside your house or shelter. When you see it coming seal that shelter. Seal every opening that will leak air. Open your door to *no one* during these days of darkness or you will perish.

Keep a small white candle burning for three days and three nights so that you will know that you are safe. This is a spiritual candle and should be blessed with a prayer. This candle will let you know when the oxygen is running low. There will be enough air inside your home or shelter for three days and three nights if you burn nothing but the candle. *(See book's survival section.)*

I pray daily that this cloud will not form, and you should also pray.

How will we prepare our children to face the future? What will they do when the machines are no longer there or not working? For this will happen. We will have to nurture them, love them and teach them spiritual values.

To survive they must know that they are loved and needed. Teach them the old ways. Love the land. Plant crops. And thank the Creator for all that we have. They *must* be taught. The Grandfathers and Grandmothers are in the children. If we teach them right, our children of tomorrow will be wiser than we are today. They are the Grandfathers and Grandmothers of tomorrow.

Some simple rules for living from the elders are these:

Native Code of Ethics

1. Each morning upon rising, and each evening before sleeping, give thanks for the life within you and for all life, for the good things the Creator has given you and others, and for the opportunity to grow a little more each day. Consider your thoughts and actions of the past day and seek for the courage and strength to be a better person. Seek for those things that will benefit everyone.

2. Respect. Respect means to "feel or show honor or esteem for someone or something; to consider the well-being of, or to treat someone or something with deference or courtesy." Showing respect is a basic law of life.

- Treat ever person from the tiniest child to the oldest Elder with respect at all times.
- Special respect should be given to Elders, parents, teachers and community Elders.
- No person should be made to feel 'put down' by you; avoid hurting others hearts as you would avoid a deadly poison.
- Touch nothing that belongs to someone else (especially sacred objects) without permission, or an understanding between you.
- Respect the privacy of every person. Never intrude on a person's quiet moments or personal space.
- Never walk between people who are conversing.
- Never interrupt people who are conversing.
- Speak in a soft voice, especially when you are in the presence of Elders, strangers, or others to whom special respect is due.

- Do not speak unless invited to do so at gatherings where Elders are present (except to ask what is expected of you, should you be in doubt).
- Never speak about others in a negative way, whether they are present or not.
- Treat the earth and all her aspects as your mother. Show deep respect for the mineral world, the plant world, and the animal world.
- Show deep respect for the beliefs and religions of others.
- Listen with courtesy to what others say, even if you feel that what they are saying is worthless. Listen with your heart.

3. Respect the wisdom of the people in council. Once you give an idea to a council or a meeting, it no longer belongs to you. It belongs to the people.

4. Be truthful at all times, and under all conditions.

5. Always treat your guests with honor and consideration. Give your best food, your best blankets, the best part of your house and your best service to your guests.

6. The hurt of one is the hurt of all. The honor of one is the honor of all.

7. Receive strangers and outsiders with a loving heart and as members of the human family.

8. All the races and tribes in the world are like the different colored flowers of one meadow. All are beautiful. As children of the Creator they must all be respected.

9. To serve others, to be of some use to family, community, nation or the world, is one of the main purposes for which human beings have been created. Do not fill yourself with your own affairs and forget your most important task. True happiness comes only to those who dedicate their lives to the service of others.

10. Observe moderation and balance in all things.

11. Know those things that lead to your well-being, and those things that lead to your destruction.

12. Listen to and follow the guidance given to your heart.

We will have to hasten back to the land and learn to be self-sufficient and attend to our spiritual welfare. We will have to learn to repair Mother Earth. And this can be done, but first we must prepare ourselves and our families for what is to come. Remember: Each one of us is responsible for our own spiritual welfare.

Great Men of this Century and Their Understanding of Mother Earth

The great hope in this century (from the 1850s) was that the magnetic field and pole reversal in all its propensity to shift would be understood and explained and predicted, which might have insured our safety. But, to my knowledge, only two non-native minds really picked up these messages sent; Edgar Cayce, whose real soul mission was to heal. He didn't truly grasp the importance of the technical data at the end. He was too worn out from the demands made on him by the thousands.

The other was Nikola Tesla. His was perhaps the most brilliant mind in that area. But he was not spiritually advanced enough to succeed in giving mankind the information. But he had it. He understood it. According to his notes, he decided to discard this information to pursue other data.

One of the things Tesla discovered about the Earth was a way to tap into the Earth's electric mantle. To go anywhere and just put a metal rod so far into the earth and, *without any other source*, have all the free electricity they wanted anywhere! He understood the Earth's own circuitry.

When a body is ill, this circuitry "misfires." The Earth's OWN electricity, coupled with the Sun, the increase in storms may cause illness or short circuiting of manmade electricity, that most arrogant extravagance, which has cost us dearly: ruining the earth with hydro-dams, exposing us to danger through nuclear power plants, just to turn on a computer.

When this short-circuit foils the computers, where will your money be? Where will your businesses be? Your food? How much of your life in the course of one day is controlled totally by electricity?

Sit down. Close your eyes. Think of your day if electricity failed. Could you even get out of your apartment or your garage?

Mankind struggled forward this last century thoroughly impressed with its own technology, which developed the seen world and ignored the unseen (or spiritual) world. This took us all on a path to doom with few real tools to survive.

Our technology has become frightening. As I have mentioned before, it is enveloping and seducing our young people. It is time that we took them away, if we can, from their machines and share with them the meaning our spiritual responsibility to each other and Mother Earth.

These messages will be a start. You can do nothing about those who will not listen (or have not listened). Do not fear this future, but rather accept it as a chance to build a better world. What you fear you bring to yourself, so walk bravely into this future. We must change our attitude and our ways.

The Eleventh Hour

*W*e are now past the eleventh hour and the time is so near that all can sense it, even the four-leggeds, even the birds and fish. Since the fall of 1996, many pets have been acting nervous.

The earth will shift three times, once almost imperceptibly, which will result in great earthquakes and volcanic activity.

The first shift causes physical unrest. The latter spiritual. Earth shifts can also cause ill health. Already asthma, sinus problems and dizziness are rampant due to this. Ear infections in children are epidemic, also.

Then a larger "lurch" will bring more flooding and increased weather changes. Watch the flooded areas closely because where the water begins to come up it eventually will rise and *not recede*. The flooding will eventually follow the areas as per the Gordon Michael Scallion *revised* map, with just a few exceptions, which will reflect the final shift.

Be mindful that the earth has an aura and the earth shifts first, then the aura shifts. Very sensitive people are already reacting physically and spiritually to these shifts.

If you live near a dam be advised that all such atrocities to our beautiful Turtle Island will break. So, if you can, move *now!*

In case of floods don't drive. Eighty per cent of all victims die in their car. Two feet of flood water can move at eighty miles per hour. Go to higher ground. Stay there. Don't try to rescue many material things or you won't get out. Plan your escape route now.

The government is well aware of the coming earth changes and, as usual, is hiding their awareness just as they have hidden so much from us personally as mature people and from all citizens (i.e. UFO cover-ups, drug cartel and more).

One thing that is happening that is important is that our water supply is being destroyed. You can live a month without food, a week without water and five minutes without air.

So far we have a so-so food supply and water that is just about poisoned. Already there is a lethal parasite growing in waters along the east coast. Already the ground water servicing many large cities is almost unfit for human consumption.

My eldest brother has fished the Great Lakes and St. Mary's River for seventy years. He has seen it go from where the whitefish ran so thick you could walk over to Canada on their backs, to where there are now hardly any fish!

Our technology camouflages these problems. In third world countries where the obvious can't be hidden, look at what's happening: Disease and starvation in Africa, famine in India, North Korea and South America.

We see this on the news and watch people dying, while we eat our overly-rich dinners and forget it by evening.

Reflect once: If these starving children were on your manicured lawn, could you eat your meal as uninvolved? If they were dying in your house, could you sleep at night without praying for them? What have we become?

Some Indicators Occurring Now and Soon to Occur
Hear And Know the Changes to Follow

- More people becoming aware of their healing gifts.

- Very young people who are wise beyond their years.

- People like us who are driven to share information with mankind.

- Disillusionment with conventional medicine and an instinctive need to seek out alternative healing.

- An urge for all people to read books like this, especially those people who have a chance to survive, whose spirits lead them to seek this knowledge.

- An increase in all, especially "sensitives," of vivid dreams. Record these immediately upon awakening and you'll see a thread running through all of them that will help you interpret them.

- One of the other signs that the people of the oceans have given us are the red tides. They are running now with more frequency.

- Place your feet flat on the floor. You can feel almost a constant electrical energy surging beneath you.

- The earth's main pulsating rate of 7.8 cycles per second has increased to 8.6 and climbing. (The Federal Aviation Authority has ordered the major airports to change their runway calibrations by ten percent due to the shift of magnetic north compass readings.)

Lisa's Prophecies

- An increase in worldwide famine.

- The door of the past in Egypt will be opened (they have already found the chamber beneath the paw of the Sphinx) and secrets will be revealed that can help us through the future.

- The comet which was referred to in many previous prophecies as the "blue star." This appears to be Hale-Bopp.

- Increase in "area-bad Karma." Bad weather for both coast lines and the mid-west. Aki, our Mother Earth is saying, "Go away from this part of me. This earth is sick and must rest under healing waters, so go away."

- In 1997-98 and '99 the weather will be very erratic, like we have never known. It will never be as it was. The summer of 1997 will have vivid thunderstorms and increased tornadoes. And this will be most difficult for large crops. Everyone should put in a small garden for staples and grow things that have a high yield. Do not depend on anything that has to be frozen. Even canning things in glass is not a good idea. During an earthquake glass will break. Grow things that can be dried or stored over a long period of time.

- In April 1999 there will be the large quake in California. It could be a 7 or 8 point quake. There will be another earthquake soon along the New Madrid Fault that runs under Chicago, Milwaukee, and up through the Keewanaw Peninsula. The last tremor on this fault was in March of 1987. Eventually there will be a quake as severe as the one in the 1800s that was so strong it rang church bells in Boston. If this happens, it could cause a vertical drop, and parts of the Upper Peninsula and the shoreline along Lake Michigan will drop down and bring tremendous disaster. It will be worse because it will be a vertical upward thrust of the plates.

I note here, though, that many of us do our spring fasts in this area and this praying and fasting appears to have kept us safe so far. So believe it that this positive energy can ameliorate things.

During the earthquakes the power will go and people in the cities will be without water, without gas, without money. And people will react with violence looking for food. Most grocery stores have about two days supply of food.

- There will be increasing severe earthquakes world-wide, as of now.

- The Hopi carvings have been explained: It is our choice as to how all this ends, as it will end differently for each one.

- Wars in the middle east and one crises after another will continue there.

- When I went with my husband to the great assembly of our people in Colorado, to the Men's Healing, way up high in the mountains, there were many prophe-cies given. And one of them was that there will be four plagues. One for each direction. Two old and two new. The old ones are possibly TB and AIDS. One of the two new ones will be called the Black Death. But this is not the "medieval" disease that was call the black plague. (Bubonic plague has already been found in the squirrel population in parts of California.) This is a new one. The nature of the fourth was not revealed to me.

- As I have said before, the earth has an aura. The Star People, they can see it at a great distance. They can see how sick the earth is now, almost in its final stages of a great illness. And the illness is humanity itself. We are dying by our own hands.

- Because the aura of the Earth is ill, and the Earth is our Mother, She will try to prevent our children from suffering. Thus sterility will increase even more than at present.

- For those who do have children, the toxic conditions we have created will result in an increase in birth defects.

- The death of Pope John Paul II. The Vatican may release the prophecies of Fatima, as they were told to do, but too far after the fact.

The long extended El Niño of 1997-98 has caused long term problems for the oceans' inhabitants. Partially caused by underwater volcanic activity, it should be a warning of all manner of Pacific Rim seismic and volcanic problems.

Where the heaviest problems have been on both coasts, the Creator is warning you all that these areas are unsafe. These coasts were the areas where our people were exterminated, and therefore, that land will be cleansed by winds and floods.

If you live near dams, consider your safety. The Mississippi has changed its course several times and will do so again. The water spirits resent being chained up!

We are all related, As is the earth is, so are we. As it is sick, so many people are now experiencing dizziness, fatigue, and cancers . . . because we live in an unnatural world with too much electricity, our immune systems are deteriorating. Germs and viruses are becoming smarter, and drugs are failing us. We have two hundred and fifty million people in the U.S. If smallpox came again, none of us are vaccinated (our childhood vaccines run out after ten years). And there is only enough vaccine available for eight million people! We have more illegal drugs than antibiotic drugs!!

We are overweight and malnourished due to junkfood and processed food. We breathe shallow because of our "couch-potato" lifestyles. Thus toxins build up. The cheapest medicine is good water, deep breathing, and the sun's caress. But we don't go outside!

If this is what our physical bodies are like, can you imagine the state of OUR SOULS?

My friends, THIS IS YOUR wake-up call. Please don't hit the snooze alarm!

Prophecies by the Elder Elders

*N*ow, hear too prophecies made by famed and respected Native Americans, some of whom lived hundreds of years ago, some in the not too distant past, and some still living.

- At the time the earth changes begin the white man will have a "cabin in the sky." (This is believed to be the space station, "Mir.")

- When one of the Kachina dancers removes his mask during a ceremonial dance the end of what we know is near. *(Hopi-Navajo)*

- The earth will speak to us through fire, earthquakes, tornados, and climatic changes. There will be large-scale evacuations of North America because earth movements will break open dams that are the source of urban energy. The cities will be plagued with blackouts, pollution, growing unemployment and soaring crime. The birth of babies malformed by chemicals will hasten the stampede back to the land and the simple life of our forefathers. Once again we will learn to be self-sufficient. Once more we will attend to our spiritual welfare. *(Dr. Adam Cuthand, Cree Nation Predictor, Saskatchewan, Canada, 1960)*

- Lake Superior used to empty out into the Mississippi. Now it empties out into the St. Lawrence. When the fish begin to disappear from the big lakes, this will reverse again. (At present the native fish are disappearing.) *(Chippewa)*

- When the top of that mountain blows off, all the west coast line is due to change just as fast, just as radically (referring to Mt. St. Helens). *(Nez Perce)*

- Our prophecies speak of these weapons (nuclear weapons). They're called the Gourd of Ashes that the white man will throw back and forth and there will be fire in the sky that no one can put out. If you don't stop what you are doing, nature will intervene. Other forces far beyond your control will come into play. The last stages are here now. All these earthquakes and volcanos and fires and hurricanes - these are the final signs, the final warnings. The last stages are here now. Our prophecies tell us in the last stages the white man will steal our lands. Its all happening now. We will pray and meditate and ask the Great Spirit to keep the world together a little longer. But it's coming. The Purifiers are coming. *(Thomas Banyacya, Sr., famed interpreter of the Hopi prophecies)*

- What's coming is already here. It's prophesied in our Instructions that the end of the world will be near when the trees start dying from the tops down. That's what the maples are doing today (1985). Our instructions say the time will come when there will be no corn, when nothing will grow in the garden, when the water will be filthy and unfit to drink. And then a great monster will rise up from the water and destroy mankind. One of the names of that monster is "the sickness that eats you up inside"—like diabetes or cancer or AIDS. Maybe AIDS is the monster. It's coming. It's already here. Our Prophet Handsome Lake told of it in the 1700s. He saw four beings, like four angels, coming from the Four Directions. They told him what would happen, how there would be diseases we'd never heard of before. You will see many tears in this country. Then a great wind will come, a wind that will make a hurricane seem like a whisper. It will cleanse the earth and return it to its original state. That will be the punishment for what we have done to the Creator. *(Chief Leon Shenandoah, "Tadodaho," Grand Council of the Six Nations Iroquois Confederacy in Upper New York)*

We are in the final stages of the shaking of the earth, when the Great Spirit takes the earth in both hands and shakes it violently. In 1993 the opening of the eastern door took place in Cape Spear, Newfoundland, Canada, the furthest eastern point in North America.

The circle of the Medicine Wheel is now complete. The Wabanaki People (People of the Light) have joined the circle. We have joined under the following philosophy: Heal you the self—you help to heal the family, the family helps to heal the nation, the nations help to heal the world. All the prophecies from other nations now coincide and compliment each other. *(David Gehue, Mic Mac Nation Spiritual Counselor)*

A New Day with New Hope

*O*ver 100 years ago, the great mystic and prophet Wowoka said a change was coming. The grass would roll over upon itself and the black earth would be exposed. The oppressors would be wiped out and the 40 million buffalo (killed in 5 to 10 years time) would come back and feed the people.

How would this happen? By means of the Spirit Dance (also called the Ghost Dance). The Ancestors would join with us and our "medicine," our spiritual helpers, the pipe, and the sweat lodge, so that we would be as we were before.

Now, had this happened, it might have been unpleasant, but we would not be at all as bad off as we are now where tremendous changes are almost unavoidable. Wowoka said, if this did not happen then, it would happen tenfold later and our people would suffer horribly in the meantime.

One of my elders said that I must include this thought: "These changes happened before. *THIS IS A NEW DAY WITH NEW HOPE. The earth survives all things because it is the Creator's earth.* Pray and prepare, but live today in the 'eternal now,' as we always have, with thanks for each day's light. If we are warned and prepared, we have *nothing to fear.* Then we can live each day to the fullest because when the time would come, we are ready."

I add to this: Don't live in fear. What you fear you bring to yourself. Being prepared disarms that fear. Being aware and prepared puts out a positive vibration for the future. If we pray and correct our mistakes perhaps the Creator will pity us and we will be spared. If the changes do occur, if we are prepared, we will survive and build a better world.

Don't despair or panic over the year 2000. Many calendars differ with this so-called Millennium. In fact, my research (published in *The Star of Bethlehem*), shows the birth of Christ to have been most likely 7 BC, which would mean we already passed the year 2000 a few years ago!

The Aftermath

*W*e will have to go back to the ways of our ancestors to survive in a good way. Many of those who survive will be very young and will learn from early-on these good ways.

This is the sunset of an old era of hatred, wars, prejudice, intolerance, soulless technology and greed. Of religion without spirituality. Of drugs, alcohol and abuse of our children. Let the sun set on all of this. Let us be purged of this. The blood of thousands of innocent victims cry out for this. All my ancestors are drumming and singing in that good land that we all go to. Let things be the way they were with all creation beautiful and clean as it was when the Great Mystery put it here.

There will be one race . . . the human race. Stop smoking and drinking *now,* so it won't be so hard on you to do it suddenly and under stress. Go up in the mountains or in the woods and fast. Accustom your body to eating less, working more.

Fasting is pleasing to the Creator. It disciplines our bodies. In the past, fasting was not only a powerful spiritual tool but it prepared us as a people for the lean times when food might not be plentiful.

Accustom your spirit to seek individual spirituality. Not the kind where groups get together and one man begins to preach to others. For only you can walk your own road to His Kingdom. No one can live for you or die for you. Learn to speak directly to the Great Mystery and learn to listen to Him for yourself.

41

Let the eye of the day close on all the chaos man have made of this good earth the Great Mystery was kind enough to put us on. Let it all pass into the night.

Surround yourself with light. Armor yourself with knowledge like that in this book. Trust in the Creator that He means us no harm. He only pities us for the great harm we have done to ourselves. Begin a true friendship with the Creator.

After the night has passed; after the long darkness when we huddle together knowing how pitiful and weak we are; after the hours of fear hearing the wind howl like marauding beasts around us . . . we will begin again. One day the sun will rise and we will still breathe. We will still hope. We will take joy in the first cry of a child being born and the laughter of our little ones. We will respect our old ones, for we need their knowledge. And a new, better and stronger world will emerge. This is the time. Let us do it right!

Physical Preparation

In our culture, the preparation of herbs for medicine is important. Years ago we never had to rely on M.D.s because we had our own "doctors." These doctors were either herbalists of great knowledge or men and women who healed through spiritual ability. Sometimes both were combined.

Learn the herbs that you can use. Leave a gift of tobacco for the plants and tell them why you are picking them. Keep a supply of brown paper bags and a ball point pen handy so that you can write the name of the herbs that have dried on the bag and pack it. Later the bags can be used for storage of other things or tinder. Do not put medicine plants in plastic. For liquids, such as bear grease, empty baby food jars can be used. Flint for fire starting is good, too, to keep handy.

Seeds are very important to save. However, the ones that you buy in the grocery store or your local nursery produce only one crop, for they are hybrids. Saving these seeds for another year is an effort in futility.

As Sun Bear wrote of his concern in *Black Dawn/Bright Day:* "In the United States and Europe, hybrid plants have been developed to produce high crop yields. But they have bred the immunities out of these plants in the process. Many of them can no longer fight off insects, molds, or other pests. Also, seeds have been developed to work best with chemical fertilizers and pesticides. Another thing to keep in mind about hybrid plants is that you can harvest the plants, but their seed is no good to plant. You have to go back to these seed companies to plant next year's crop. So the seeds, in reality are owned by multinational corporations. Since these companies have a monopoly on hybrid seeds, farmers are finding that prices are going up every year. It is very frightening that we are dependent on gasoline driven engines and petroleum-based chemicals for our farming. I look around and wonder what will happen when there is no petroleum . . . this is a very dangerous time because we are totally dependent on oil companies for our food supply, and they are largely dependent on oil from the Middle East."

I seriously suggest that you write to a company like Bountiful Gardens for their seed catalog which is free. The address is on page 90. They produce seeds and plants that are *non-hybrid* and grown without chemical fertilizers and pesticides. These seeds you CAN save for next year's crop.

Seeds are very important to save, because, if enough volcanic activity occurs, the climate will change more and we may have one season where nothing grows. A good supply of dirt, once you are in a secure place, and some seeds can start a lot of plants early to replenish the earth. Especially sage, cedar, sweet grass and tobacco seeds should be on hand. These are the four sacred medicines. They heal by spiritual means, and the cedar makes a wonderful tea, which is purifying as well as medicinal. (We don't pick cedar in the rain or at night, and it is usually only picked by women.) Medicine plants should not be washed, unless they are roots.

If you have a lot of fine seeds, like radishes, the sprouts are good.

A safe, nourishing liquid, clear and pure, is maple sap, and it's available in the spring from our good brothers, the trees.

For native people, spiritual needs must be met. Most of us with pipes will pass those on.

Sweat lodges can be readily constructed (as can shelters for living space) from a few poles and coverings. A couple of dark tarps or several large black plastic garbage bags should be packed for this purpose. A spool of sinew is going to be needed, too, to secure the lodge poles. Sinew can make a good rabbit snare, too.

Each nation usually knows the plants in its area or edible roots. In the old days we had many winters where near-famine prevailed.

In preparation for a repeat of tough times remember to do your spring and fall fasts. Fast often during the year, one to four days, to discipline your body. While the sweat lodge is the place to speak to the Creator, fasting is a listening prayer. Use this time to listen and watch for signs, even for visions.

It would be best to taper off all the bad habits now. Alcohol is not to be a part of traditional life for it drives away one's spirit; diminishes it. Try to rid yourself of cigarettes, sugar and other addictions. It will improve your body now and should these things suddenly become un-available it will make the transition easier.

Seek out your elders and traditional people now and learn all you can from them. Remember to offer tobacco before you ask a question.

Regarding tobacco: be sure to have enough on hand. This is the first plant created by the Great Mystery and this is why it is welcomed by Him as an offering. Most traditional people know how to enlarge the tobacco supply by taking the green inner bark of the willow, drying it and adding it to your tobacco along with bear-berry leaves. Such plants can double your tobacco supply. Only a pinch is needed as an offering.

Spiritual Preparation

Although these changes seem inevitable, the final word will belong to the Creator. For year the "light workers" have been told to move to certain points to reinforce the grid work or power points on Mother Earth. These are similar to the acupuncture points on the human body. These "light workers" were to lead good lives (especially to avoid alcohol), pray and draw positive energy to these areas.

In the non-native world, Mary apparitions and Angel appearances abound, all giving the same information: prepare for the changes, pray that the changes aren't harsh, improve your actions and life styles. My dear adopted grandmother, Grandma Julie, saw who I believe to be Mary many times. She never presumed to say it was Mary and just called the young woman "the beautiful Lady."

Grandma Julie first saw the Lady when she was five years old. Ever since then, when she was troubled, the

Lady would appear. The Lady was about 16 or 17, slender, with wavy blondish brown hair. Her gown was simple, and sometimes she wore a veil. She had a golden-brown (but light) complexion. Julie couldn't described the eyes because when she looked at the Lady's eyes, such emotion flooded her being, such a feeling of love, that her eyes welled with tears of joy and blurred.

The Lady never spoke, just smiled and showed her things that would happen.

One time during the depression, the family had no money, and Grandma Julie was just a girl. She walked along the snowy street and turned the corner. There on the snowbank sat the "beautiful Lady." Julie smiled, and the Lady smiled back and handed her a sprig of cedar with three leaf clumps. At once Julie "knew" she would have work for three weeks—just in time for Christmas. When she looked up, the Lady was gone.

When she went in the back door of the old house where they lived, her mother said they should both go right away to the local factory because seamstresses were needed for three weeks' work to finish a big order they had!

The Lady was always there for Grandma. She and other good and gentle spirits are always there for all of us if we believe.

Pray and meditate. Trust in the Creator. These, too, are our survival tools. The preparation for what to bring with you should you have to relocate suddenly to a safe place, differs for each religion. As for native people this is simpler.

Most of us traditional people keep all our "sacred items" in a bag or a bundle. We store all the medicines in one place so that we will be able to pick them up quickly.

Final Visions

Again, as I slept, the dream teacher came. For several nights the dear old woman was sitting on the moss covered log with the huge mossy boulders all around that looked like ancient turtles had come to visit. Shafts of sunlight tried to dance down to us through the great white pines as she showed me, among other things, a new beadwork pattern for my sister Barb.

But this night it was the old man. He seemed to be carved out of pipestone. Two points of light in his dark eyes shone out of his face. He had his pipe with him, smoking on the things we talked about. Deep in thought, while the blue smoke rolled out of his mouth on either side of the stem and drifted up to the Creator.

We were on a smooth rounded grandfather rock as large as a house, with lichen here and there until the forest took over. One side was open and I could see the brilliant blue of Lake Superior shining in the distance. Ancient petroglyphs covered the rock.

He finished the pipe and sat with his eyes closed. I waited. Was he listening to his spirit messengers? Was he napping? Was he just seeing how polite and patient I could be? Probably all of the above! I waited.

"If we would have turned it all around years ago as the prophets told us to, many lives would have been spared and this Turtle Island would have been a jewel in the water. These teachings were scattered and lost. So it is all happening after all.

"But the Great Mystery showed me this new world to come and it was a good place to be. He had to stop what we were doing! It will take 100 years for the forest and the four-leggeds to be as they should.

"It will take 1000 years for the water to be as it once was.

"And it will take 10,000 years for the earth to purge itself of the poisons put into her.

"But this is only time. In the history of this earth these numbers mean little.

"People will get through this all. Mankind will survive. Babies will be born. Children will grow up. They will miss none of the material things we mourn because they will only know what they have.

"It will be a better world coming.

"We have been made to start over many times by the Creator, we just don't have the remembrance of all those times.

"He is a good Father

"The Earth is a good Mother.

"But, we were not the best of children!

"He always gives us another chance. He is patient and kind and loving.

"Never forget this: You have a good Father. A good Mother. Be a good Child to them and everything will be alright."

I woke up. The birds were singing the sun's wake up songs. I went outside and raised a pinch of tobacco in my left hand to it. I thanked the four directions, the Creator and Mother Earth for this good day and placed the offering by our cedar trees.

I am glad to be alive.

I will be glad to go 'home' someday to join my ancestors and the Creator in the Land of Beauty and Light. And, in between, I'll be a good Child, prepared and alert but not afraid to hold onto each day's gifts.

It was Monday night, May 15, 1997, and I had just settled down into bed after smudging with sweet grass and sage. I felt very comfortable, but was not asleep.

Suddenly, I heard water gurgling and, before I knew it, I was in a car near the higher section of the International Bridge (the one that goes between Sault Ste. Marie, Ontario and Sault Ste. Marie, Michigan). It seemed to be about eleven at night and a warm evening. I felt that it must be about August or early September. I noticed that the lights on the bridge were out.

Now, this is most curious because this is an international bridge between two countries and the lights are always on. I looked at the water below me. The rapids were no longer there and the water was moving powerfully and rushing out towards the lower lakes at a tremendous rate . . . deep and swift, it had become an expanse that looked almost as wide as the Mississippi River!

I looked toward the Canadian side of the river (the St. Mary's River) and the water was so high that the board-walk lights along the shore were glowing beneath the water and most of the city lights on the Canadian side were out.

I was in the car we now own, which we hope will last another five years.

I feel that this is a forewarning of flooding that will happen sooner than expected. There is such a sense of urgency with this vision that I felt nauseated. I knew that I should let everyone know so that they could prepare.

Other people from this area have confided similar experiences. One spoke of seeing houseboats by Brimley (north of Sault Ste. Marie, Michigan) in a dream. The boats were anchored over areas where their houses had once been on land.

Meeting the Challenge

Survival Guidelines
and Sound Advice for Providing
Shelter, Food, and Health Care
During the Coming Changes

*A*s Elisabeth and I talked together of her visions and strong need to share these prophecies and guidance, we came to believe, also, that very specific help in survival techniques should be included. That is what is offered in the following pages.

A few years ago I published a manual called *Mayday*. It was and is a good basic guide for gathering, storing and preparing for basic human and animal needs in order to survive disasters. We decided to selectively reprint it here, with editing and additions by each of us. As you can tell from the following Author's Notes, we two women may come from different places (in this life) yet were sisters before we met!

—Shirley Jonas

Author's Notes

Sir William Osler once said, "Humanity has but three great enemies: fever, famine and war." I would add to this—tornadoes, hurricanes, forest fires, earthquakes, floods, and *ourselves!* Many people are beginning to realize that this world is rapidly moving towards a very uncertain future. We ask ourselves, "What can we do about it?"

At the rate our government is going, it does seem that we are pretty much on our own. Somewhere along the way, we have lost touch with the "powers that be" in political office (if we were ever in touch with them at all) and they have forgotten about us.

And, generally speaking, we have lost touch with who we really are and what we have done and are doing to Mother Earth. I say, too, that Mother Earth is starting to fight back. All over the world we are having violent storms, hurricanes, tornadoes, floods, earthquakes and forest fires where there have seldom been these things before. Not only are these cataclysmic events happening more frequently, but they are increasing in intensity.

I have had the experience of being snowed in, with my young family, for three days on two occasions . . . no power . . . no furnace heat . . . no telephone. When the snow plows finally got through, we were rather disappointed! For three days we had been on our own, cooking over the fireplace, lighting the house with candles and oil lamps and all of us snuggling down at night in our sleeping bags in the living room. Before bedtime we read, played games and got to know each other again, minus the TV and the radio. The kids thought it was a great adventure.

Then we moved to Alaska for a while. Now *there* is a place that one *has* to know about being prepared for almost anything. The long summers were wonderful, but when the mercury dipped to forty below in the winter, we had to be prepared both in our home and on the road. A person's vehicle needed emergency equipment in the trunk, and I don't mean an extra tire jack!

Those experiences may have been the seed from which this section of the book has grown. The pages that follow are meant to assist you in making sure that you and your loved ones will feel more secure and as comfortable as possible, no matter what lies ahead.

What kind of a position would you be in to handle an emergency tomorrow? What if you and your family faced something far worse than just three days in a snow storm, being stranded on an Alaskan Highway in the winter, or a forest fire evacuation?

What if there were no Salvation Army or Red Cross to help you out? Could you keep warm, eat well, and be able to cope with emergencies such as a cut finger, snake bite, burns, or even a broken arm or leg?

You can be prepared. Follow this book TO THE LETTER. We all tend to be procrastinators, especially on sunny days. A number of years ago I sent away for a manual flour mill. I wanted to grind my own flour. I remember the tag on that big box from Utah. It said, "Remember: It wasn't raining when Noah built the Ark!"

And I say to you, in all seriousness, DO IT NOW. What has been written in this book is from true hearts and people of wisdom. It is not meant in any way to be a "scare tactic." Our world is changing rapidly. A lot of it will be for the better, but meanwhile we may have to take care of ourselves and each other.

First Moves In "Natural" Disasters

Quite some time ago when we lived in a small town in northern California we were asked to evacuate in a hurry from our home because of a terrible forest fire. We were told by the sheriff deputies to head for the fairgrounds 10 miles away. With 30 minutes in which to gather the family and pets, make decisions and proceed calmly up the road—this real emergency became a "test run" for some of the advice that follows.

For many people, panic arrives with evacuation orders. If you are not in a ready mode you will quickly become aware that panic shuts your brain down. You look around your house wondering what to grab first and discover that what you cannot find is your mind.

I'm sure this happened to many people caught in the floods that hit North and South Dakota and Minnesota this year. If you watched these terrible disasters on TV, did you say to yourself, "I wonder what I would do if this happened to us?" What if an earthquake hit, or a volcano erupted and you were *there?* Are you ready?

ORGANIZE NOW! I'm not saying pack up your house. I'm saying have your car gassed up at all times, with extra gas in a can because you never know how far you'll need to go, and what you need packed and easy to grab. Do your thinking now so that you can move safely and automatically when the time comes.

In most cases there's a lot you will have to leave behind. Sit down now and make what I call a "skinny list." Put it on your fridge door. Sit quietly and decide what you can grab in a hurry that means the most to you. Go over the list again and make it "skinny." Show the list to your family and allocate the items that they are each responsible for and where they are located.

If you are by yourself, list only what you can carry in one suitcase or plastic bag.

On the next several pages I have listed what to have in the trunk of your car or in the back of your truck, plus what you can store in the house in one place that is packed with emergency things for living in the wild, if need be, for a period of time.

And don't laugh. This can happen! If your home becomes uninhabitable you can camp out in relative comfort if you are prepared. All schools and some businesses have a fire drill once in a while. So let's call this a fire drill.

Have in your home, in a convenient place, what I call a "grab and run container." This is a clean plastic garbage can packed with everything you will need for a while. It really is quite simple to be ready for almost anything. The illustration below will show you how to pack it and the list following will give you some idea of what to pack. This container can easily be stored in a corner, a closet or a garage.

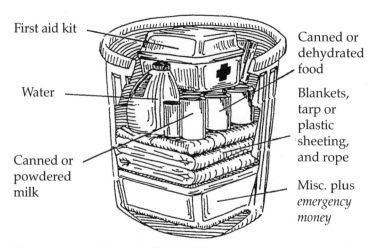

First aid kit

Water

Canned or powdered milk

Canned or dehydrated food

Blankets, tarp or plastic sheeting, and rope

Misc. plus *emergency money*

Grab and Run container:**

First aid kit	Flashlight
Water	(with extra batteries)
Candles	Waterproof matches
(with holders)	Fire starter package*
Toilet paper	Canned heat
Dehydrated food	Backpacker's mess kit
Space blankets	Tarp or plastic sheet
6" Hunting knife	Rope
Roll of aluminum foil	Hatchet
Dry kindling	Plastic garbage bags
Maps	Pet food (dry)
Portable water filter	*Duct Tape*
(hand pump style)	

*To prepare a simple but very efficient fire starter kit : Take a package of cotton balls and knead petroleum jelly (Vaseline) into each one. Place in plastic bag and seal. This works far better than dry twigs (if you can find them) or newspaper. Just light a cotton ball, place under kindling and your fire will soon blaze!

**This is a basic list for immediate temporary needs. You and your family may have other "must have" items, such as medicine, that you will add at the last moment.

Looking for a Safe Area

You have already read what Elisabeth Dietz has suggested about areas that flood easily and perhaps this will increase in those areas and you should look for high ground and stay there.

Many years ago Edgar Cayce suggested the following: "That the safety lands will be portions of Ohio, Indiana and Illinois, and much of the southern portion of Canada and the eastern portion of Canada, while the western land, much of that is to be disturbed."

I suggest that you write to: Matrix Institute, Inc., P. O. Box 336, Chesterfield, NH 03443-0336. Or phone their customer service number: (603) 363-4916.

Ask for the REVISED Future Map of North America, which includes the contingent United States of America, Alaska and Hawaii, plus Mexico and Central America.

I think there are two serious matters to consider with regard to a "safe" area. One should be uppermost in your mind . . . get away from any large city . . . as far away as possible. Secondly, if it is at all possible, buy land—enough to plant and harvest a large garden, provide underground water** and supply some fuel. Depending on the size of your family, one acre could work but five acres is best.

I have friends that got together and bought forty acres complete with an old but adequate farm house. Perhaps you can get together with like-minded people if you are short in the money department. (Aren't we all?)

**This is where learning to dowse comes in handy. See section on "necessary books."

Vehicle Mini-survival Kit

Keep the following in your garage, your car trunk or in a waterproof box in the back of your truck. This list is an expansion of the "grab and run" container. If possible, prepare *both*. You and your vehicle may not be at home when disaster strikes, or *you* may be at home without your vehicle.

Nonperishable <u>food</u> in sealed packages, or clean coffee cans

Bottled water

Backpacker water purification system (a must have)

First aid kit and book (with herbal and natural remedy information) and your family's essential medications

Personal hygiene items (soap, tooth brush, sanitary napkins, diapers)

Break lights (see source list at back of this book)

Sleeping bags, blankets or space blankets

Sealable plastic bags

Flashlight with extra batteries

Tools (screwdrivers, pliers, hammer, axe, bow saw, sharpening file, fox hole folding shovel, wrenches)

Short, small rubber tubing for siphoning

Local and state maps

Extra clothes for winter, summer, rain

Sturdy shoes (hiking boots)

Tent or very large tarp

Garbage bags

Waterproof matches

Fire starter and kindling

Two can openers

Candles

Rope and twine

Thread, pins, needles

Hunting knives (fillet, ulu, 6" steel blade)

Metal plates, cups, forks and spoons

Mess kit and/or cooking pans

Battery operated or spring wound clock

Portable radio and extra batteries

Emergency Shelters for All Seasons Camping Equipment and Supplies

One never knows when a temporary shelter may turn into a permanent camp. For those who have very little experience with camping, the following should help.

When setting up a camp, keep in mind the following: camp uphill and dig your latrine downhill. Don't camp too close to the trees, but make sure there are enough trees in the area to supply you with wood for building shelters. Use dead wood for fires and use this wood sparingly.

If the weather is chilly put on more clothes. Layering your clothing provides more warmth.

Camp away from the water to protect your camp from rising water caused by rain and melting snow.

Keep waste to a minimum. Bury what waste you accumulate downhill and deep, away from your campsite. Furry little things like garbage . . . and even BIG furry things!

Always put water taken from streams or lakes through a portable water purifying system. Besides other environmental hazards, there is a tiny little critter called "binucleated flagellate protozoan parasite," commonly know as Giardia. NOT FILTERING your water is an invitation to this nasty parasite to offer you "heaves" and painful diarrhea, plus fever. It loves the lining of your intestines. Up north we call this "Beaver Fever." Have I convinced you?

Add to your packing list (for "grab and run" or vehicle) the following items that may not be essential but will add to your comfort and convenience:

- Fishing poles, lures, hooks and line

- Rifle and ammunition (for wild game as well as protection)
- Pencils, paper, crayons
- Books, games and playing cards.
- Whittling knife (to make pegs to hold things together or in place. Holes can be made by whittling, burning and boring with a stick.)

Books You Should Have with You

- First Aid

- Herbal Remedies (Choose a book with clear instructions on how to prepare harvested herbs for use, as well as good photos for identification. The Books and Periodicals chapter has some suggestions)

- *Stalking the Blue Eyed Scallop* by Euell Gibbons. (This one is great for finding food in the woods. You'll be surprised at the delicious things that grow in the woods around you! I called the bookstore and they do have a reprint of this book and they stock other field guides on edible wild plants . . . as well as guidebooks on poisonous plants.)

- Write to (or call) B&A Products, Rt # 1, Box 100, Bunch, Oklahoma 74931-9705 and ask Byron for the United States Army Survival Manual. (No one knows survival better than the Army!) While you are at it, ask him to send you a free copy of their catalog. If you can't find it in this catalog with regard to emergency preparedness, it might not have been invented yet!

Emergency Shelters in Snow

(1) Heap and pack snow in a pile. Here and there, shove branches into the packed snow.

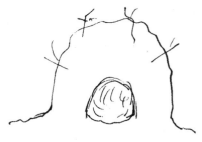

(2) Hollow out a small opening away from the wind. The twigs will hold it together. Throw evergreen branches on the "floor."

(3) Curl up inside. The evergreens will keep you off the ground. The R-factor of the snow should keep the interior at 50 degrees.

Shelters for Spring and Summer

   (1) Select a frame type.

Select a higher ground spot NOT under the trees, on level ground. Bend or break several branches. Use rope, strong twine, vines or pieces ripped from your clothes to tie them. Spread pine boughs on the ground inside. Fire is kept outside. Face opening away from the wind.

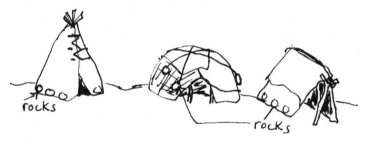

(2) Cover with blankets. Lace tepee by shoving sharp sticks through material. Weigh down edges with rocks.

(3) If you packed a tarp, cover the blankets with that to waterproof. If you have neither tarp or blankets, use birch bark, bark or pine boughs to cover the frame. If you have the time, use *all poles* and pack with clay or mud.

Temporary Emergency Food Supplies for One Person for One Month

Water: If you are in a permanent place you should have two gallons of water per person. Store in well-cleaned, tightly covered containers such as thermos jugs or plastic bottles. Change water once a month or have water purification tablets on hand, or a portable water purifying system.

Food:

- 28 cans evaporated milk (16 oz)
- 8 cans apple juice (20 oz)
- 8 cans orange juice (10 oz)
- 8 cans peaches (10 oz)
- 4 cans peas (10 oz)   + Beans
- 8 cans tomatoes (20 oz)
- 14 individual size cold cereal (that form bowls when opened)
- 8 cans corn beef (7 oz)
- 4 cans lunch meat (12 oz)
- 4 cans salmon/tuna (3 ½ oz)
- 4 boxes soda crackers (1 lb)
- 12 cans baked beans (single serving)
- 4 small jars cheese
- 4 cans vegetable soup
- 1 large can/jar of honey
- 4 small plastic jars peanut
- 4 lbs hard candy
- butter
- 4 small boxes sugar
- 4 small boxes tea bags

4 jars instant coffee (2 oz)
Salt and pepper
4 cans of butter (1 lb)
Powdered milk (large box)

Alternative or additional items (if you choose):
  Canned carbonated beverages
  Grapefruit, lemon, tomato juice in individual cans
  Applesauce (canned)
  Green beans (canned)
  Corn (canned)
  Instant potatoes
  Pre-cooked cereal (instant type)
  Graham crackers
  Melba toast
  Canned gravy
  Sardines
  Dehydrated soups (such as the kind that come in
    Styrofoam cups and all you add is hot water)
  Jam, jelly, marmalade, syrup, molasses
  Instant chocolate powder
  Instant rice
  Pancake mix
  Pastas

Special requirements for children
  For each infant, include:
    28 cans of evaporated milk (16 oz)
    12 gallons of water
    infant food and formula
  For each child up to three years, include:
    8 large cans milk
    6 gallons of water

Large Storage for Permanent Safe Area

Now, if you feel that you want to go into storage in a big way and you are in a safe permanent area, and have a clean, cool dry place in your basement with adequate storage shelves, or a dry, cool place in your yard, the following items will take care of your family for a long time. *Keep in mind that this is a checklist. You no doubt have much of this in your home already.*

To assist you in the number of items and container sizes, use amount guide on pages 62–63. *64 - 65*

Apple butter

Asparagus

Apples (dehydrated)

Apricots (dehydrated)

Baking powder

Bisquick mix

Brown sugar

Beans (dry; pinto or navy)

Canned fruit

Beets

Baked beans

Beef stew

Bouillon (beef and chicken granules—less expensive than cubes)

Beef jerky

Corn starch

Cocoa

Drink mixes (powdered)

Dry potatoes (can or box)

Eggs (whole powdered)

Flour (in metal containers with tight lids!)

Gelatin (sweet or unsweetened)

Honey

Jams and jellies

Maple flavoring (for making syrup)

Macaroni and noodle meals (box or can)

Margarine and canned butter

Onions (minced dry)

Powdered milk

Pepper

Corn meal
Canned corn
Canned meat (include
   sandwich spreads)
Carrots (canned)
Cabbage (canned)
Cheese (powdered cheddar)
SaltShortening (can or bottle)
Seasonings
Sugar
String beans
Soups (liquid or dry)
Spinach
Spaghetti
Spaghetti dinners (can
   or box)
Wheat, dark hard winter
   cleaned for human consumption
Cracked wheat, soybeans, other grains

Peas (canned or dry)
Pork and beans
Peanut butter
Peaches
Pears
Rice (regular or instant)
Raisins

Salmon
Tomatoes
Tomato juice
Tuna
Vanilla
Vinegar
Vitamins (mega-multiple
   and vitamin C)

Note 1. Unless otherwise noted, all above vegetables, fruit and liquid items are canned.

Note 2. Do not store directly on concrete floors. Put up on raised planks or shelves and use rodent-proof metal cans.

Other storage items:

CLEANING:
Ammonia
Lysol disinfectant (concentrate)
Hand soap (unwrap, so it becomes
   "hard-milled" and lasts longer)
Washing soap
Cleaning rags
Towels, cloth and paper

Bleach (also useful
   for purifying water)
Cleanser
Scrubbing brush
   and broom
Water purification
   tablets
Portable water filter

HARDWARE:
Fishing poles, hooks, lures, and line
Inflatable boat with bicycle pump
Axe, army type collapsible shovel, and garden tools
Saw (handsaw and bow saw), chain saw, and fuel mix
Tarp and plastic sheeting
Aluminum foil
Heat cubes or canned heat with stand
Assorted nails and screws, set of screwdrivers, and pliers
Heavy-duty staple gun and refills
Crescent wrench (for turning off gas main among other
    things)
Hammer, wire cutters, wrenches, crowbars (set)
Flashlight and extra batteries
Large water container (plastic garbage can with lid)
Small metal barrel wood stove and stove pipe (see
    Lehman's Non-Electric Catalog)
Kindling wood
Rifle and shells
Metal wastebaskets
Candles
Waterproof matches
Fire extinguisher (A.B.C. type)
Rope (all sizes, cotton, hemp, and nylon) and duct tape
Coil of baling wire
Powdered chlorinated lime (add to sewage to deodorize,
    disinfect and keep away insects)
Coleman stove and fuel**
Coleman lamps (with extra socks)**
Coleman portable oven
Oil lamps with extra chimneys
Lamp oil (extra wicks)
** Never use camp stoves or other petroleum-fueled items
indoors . . . only candles and oil lamps. Any fuel-burning lamp
or stove burns oxygen, and may explode if the mixture is not
right. Use them outdoors.

PERSONAL ITEMS:
Personal prescription drugs or alternative herbal
    substitutes
Toilet tissue
Deodorant
Razors
Tooth paste and brushes (baking soda can be substituted
    for paste)
Shaving cream (hand soap can be substituted for this)
Shampoo
Combs and brushes
90% UV protection sunglasses
Shoe laces
Sanitary napkins (non-deodorant type can also be used
    for pressure bandages)
Diapers for baby (Regular cotton type that can be boiled
    and reused and can also be used for many other needs)
Other personal toilet items
Clothing—think ahead! It may be summer, but where
    are winter clothes? sweaters, socks, gloves, coats, wool
    hats, scarves, and boots.
Blankets and sleeping bags

KITCHEN ITEMS:
Cooking utensils—stainless steel or cast iron—
    NO ALUMINUM
Grocery bags
Plastic garbage bags, assorted sizes
Waterproof matches
Baby supplies (bottles, etc)
Bottled water
Two can openers
Measuring dropper
Measuring spoons
Sharp knives

Manual flour mill
Manual grinder for meats, fruits, vegetables and nuts
   (See Lehman's catalog)
Silverware, metal plates, metal cups, metal bowls
Candles, paraffin
Needles, pins, safety pins
Thread (fine and carpet)
Buttons and hooks
Scissors

NOTES ABOUT SELECTING STORAGE ITEMS:

- If you are in a *permanent* place, choose foods that will keep and store easily.
- Consider family preferences and individual appetites and needs (such as low-salt diets)
- Select foods in cans or sealed packages. Glass will break in an earthquake.
- Where you have limited space or have to move or travel, buy some freeze dried foods or dehydrated food.
- Select foods that require little or no preparation.
- If you are in your permanent place, date foods when purchased or rotate it through normal use.
- Turn cans of evaporated milk, end to end, every three months to prevent curdling. This should also be done with baby formula.
- Keep all foods in a cool, dry place.
- Store some quantity of extra food or goods for use in trade. There may come a time when currency will be of little value!
- If you are in your vehicle and have to abandon it, select foods that are not heavy to carry in a backpack. (See special section under "mini-survival kit.")
- Always use candles in safe holders. Anything that can tip over and cause a fire should be fastened down securely.

Some long-range precautions:

In addition to temporary emergency supplies, we should think about being self-sufficient from a long range standpoint as well. In case of a complete national emergency or natural disaster, depend on *yourself.*

One of the most essential things to provide is safe, clean water. We cannot live without water. In a disaster, the public supply will be contaminated. Even lakes and streams will be unsafe. Prepare for this by having water supplies and ways of cleansing water (as given in preceding lists) the number one items in importance!

If you stay permanently in your home, shut off the outside gas *and* the water supply that comes into your home. Even outside wells, if you have one, probably won't be safe. If it is a deep well, and you have electrical power, you'll be okay using your well, but it would be safer to use a means of purification. You can also sterilize water by the following method. *This should be done right away for long term storage.*

Fill clean jars up to one inch from top. Put on lids and rings and process them in your canner (boiling hot water bath, such as you do when canning juices.) Boil quart size 20 minutes, two quart size 25 minutes. Remove and tighten seal and place on rack to cool.

Glass jars can break easily, so place them on wood planks against a wall or anywhere they will be protected. Cushion them with spare blankets or towels. Place boards over the top.

You should store seeds. Purchase them in vacuum packed cans, usually from a store that sells dehydrated and freeze dried foods. Call or visit your local health food store. Remember, this is a long term situation. Use your seeds sparingly the first year. One fourth of your garden crop should be stored for seed or allowed to go to seed.

You'll be running out of your seed storage supply, if you don't. Always keep one fourth of the seeds in storage in case a crop is lost to insects or unfavorable weather.

A Simple First Aid Box for Emergency Storage

1 bottle of mild antiseptic to clean cuts (3% hydrogen peroxide)

Antibiotic first aid ointment

5 yards of 2 inch gauze bandage

2 triangular bandages to use for slings

1 packet paper tissue (such as Kleenex)

Twelve 4" by 4" sterile pads to cover cuts, wounds or burns

12 assorted individual 'bandaids'

2 small bottles of insect repellant

2 large dressing pads, 8" x 8" size

5 yards ½ inch adhesive tape

One package of safety pins

1 small bottle of tooth ache drops or clove oil

1 tube of petroleum jelly

1 small bottle children's non-aspirin pain killer (never give aspirin to anyone under the age of 16)

1 small bottle of aspirin for those who can tolerate it

1 small bottle of non-aspirin pain killer, adult strength

1 thermometer

1 pair small blunt end scissors

1 pair tweezers

Assortment of small embroidery needles (extra sharp) and cotton thread, heavy duty. These items can be boiled to sterilize and used to suture, if a long-term situation develops.

1 box baking soda

1 small jar multiple vitamins

1 small jar vitamin C (very important)

1 First Aid Manual
U.V sun protection cream—highest number
(See page 75 for Herbal First Aid Kit)

Medical Supplies for Large Permanent Storage

Check list—most of these are in your home already

Aspirin, Anacin, or Tylenol (Aspirin given to those
   under 16 may cause Reyes Syndrome)
Alcohol or other disinfectant fluid
Aloe vera gel (for burns and sores)
Anti-itch ointment (also see herbal remedies for this)
Antibiotic first aid ointment (also see herbal remedies
   for this)
Butterfly clamps
Box of assorted adhesive bandages
Baking soda
Bath and hand towels
Bed sheets
Bed pan
Calamine lotion
Pepto Bismol (the "bismol" in this has been known to
   help heal ulcers)
Cod liver oil
Codeine (order through doctor)
Creomulsion Natural Cough Medicine (in Canada—
   Buckley's Mixture. Also, see herbal remedies)
Bag Balm
Disinfectant spray
Epsom salts
Eye wash preparation
Flashlight and extra batteries
FIRST AID BOOK
Hot water bottle

Household chlorine solution (for purification of water)
Hypodermic needles for special cases such as diabetes
Hydrogen peroxide
Imodium AD
Kaopectate for diarrhea (see herbal remedies also)
Lysol disinfectant (plastic bottle)
Milk of magnesia
Measuring cup
Measuring spoons
Needles (can be heated to sterilize)
Oil of Cloves for tooth ache
Oral thermometer
Roll of gauze bandages (2" wide)
Roll of adhesive tape (1" wide)
Roll of absorbent cotton (sterile)
Single edge razor blades
Rubbing alcohol
Sterile gauze dressings 4"x4" square
Scissors
Sling
Snake bite kit
Package assorted safety pins
Straight pins
Splints
Table salt
Toilet tissue
Toilet soap
Tongue depressors
Tourniquet or pressure bandage
Tweezers
Vicks Vaporub
Vitamins (high potency for medicinal use)
Wood safety matches (waterproof)

Homeopathic and/or Herbal First Aid

Most of the following can be ordered (initially) from your health food store and, if they don't have it in stock, ask them to order the items. For long term self-reliance, learn to grow, gather and process all that you can. See suggested books in following chapter.

Comfrey Ointment—speeds healing

Chickweed cream—helps draw out splinters . . . also for burns

Calendula (or Marigold cream)—antiseptic and anti-fungal for cuts and scrapes

Tea Tree Oil—highly antiseptic and anti-fungal, for cuts, warts, and cold sores

Arnica tablets—for domestic shocks or accidents. 1 tablet at 30-minute intervals. Also used for nosebleeds.

Apis tablets—for bee stings. 30C every 15 minutes for up to 6 doses.

Poison ivy first aid: rinse affected area with apple cider vinegar and goldenseal. Apply poultice of equal parts witch hazel, mugwort, white oak bark, and plantain. Then apply aloe vera gel for itching.

Headaches: Evening Primrose Oil Capsules. 3 to 4 at breakfast and again at dinner. Take herbs—feverfew for migraines as well as ginkgo biloba.

Eucalyptus leaves—Pour boiling water over a few leaves (or simmer) and inhale steam for chest infections.

Yarrow—same use as above

Backache: Massage with camphorated oil, then apply
   hot wool compress or hot moist compress of water
   and apple cider vinegar.
Sore throat: For infection, chew a small piece of Oshe
   Root. Also, gargle with an infusion of sage, ginger tea,
   or slippery elm tea.
Gastric Upsets: Echinacea and Goldenseal.
   Teas—chamomile, comfrey or slippery elm.
Papaya—for indigestion.

If we have to do without hospitals, we have to consider
living cautiously. Keeping clean will prevent a lot of ill-
nesses and infections. Not eating seeds from cucumbers or
tomatoes will prevent appendicitis. Find out what the
local natives used for the Big Three: heart disease, cancer,
and diabetes. Around here, we have foxglove, which has
natural digitalis and "Swamp Tea," which cleanses arteries
and lowers cholesterol. Strawberry root tea is also a heart
tonic if picked after it blossoms and before berries are ripe.

Many years of research proved out seventy-five percent or better help in treating cancer with Lasagnen, now
known as Essiac Tea. But only if made as follows:

ESSIAC (in Ojibway: Lasagnen)
Supplies needed:
   4 or 5 gallon stainless steel pot
   2 gallon stainless steel pot with lid
   Stainless steel fine-mesh double strainer
   Stainless steel funnel
   Stainless steel spatula
   12 or more 16 ounce amber glass bottles with air
tight caps (not childproof caps)
   2 gallons of sodium-free distilled water

Essiac Formula

    6.5 cups burdock root, cut (Artium Lappa)

    16 oz. sheep sorrel herb, powdered (Rumex Acetosella)

    1 oz. turkey rhubarb root, powdered (Rheum Palmatum)

    4 oz. slippery elm bark, powdered (Ulmus Fulva)

Preparation

    1. Mix Essiac formula thoroughly.

    2. Bring sodium-free distilled water to a rolling boil in a 5-gallon pot with lid on. (Approximately 30 minutes at sea level.)

    3. Stir in 1 cup of Essiac formula. Replace lid and continue boiling for 10 minutes.

    4. Turn off stove. Scrape down sides of pot with spatula and stir mixture thoroughly. Replace lid.

    5. ?

    6. Turn off stove. Strain liquid into 3-gallon pot, and clean 5-gallon pot and strainer. Then strain filtered liquid back into 5-gallon pot.

    7. Use funnel to pour hot liquid into bottles immediately, taking care to tighten caps. Allow bottles to cool; then tighten the caps again.

    8. Refrigerate. Essiac contains no preservative agents. If mold should develop in the bottle, discard immediately.

Wash all bottles well for reuse

Directions for Use:

    Heat four tablespoons (2 oz.) sodium-free distilled water in a stainless steel pot. Add 4 tablespoons of Essiac (shake bottle first). Mix and drink.

Take at bedtime on an empty stomach, at least 2 hours after eating.

All of these suggestions are for times when medical help is unavailable and should only be used if the user studies herbs and has no allergies. Always take a small dose to "test" your reactions.

Questions regarding Essiac Tea (Lasagnen) recipe and dosage, information on how to obtain a good source of herbs, to purchase the book, or other questions, please contact: Dr. Gary L. Glum, c/o Silent Walker Publishing, P.O. Box 92856, Los Angeles, CA 90009. Phone: 310-271-9931.

A simple remedy from our area helps diabetes:

DIABETES HERBAL
(This medicine requires specific instructions per individual use and close glucose monitoring.)
Ingredients:
    1 cup yarrow
    3 cones stahorn sumac
    1½ gallons mineral or spring water
    1 cup blueberry leaves
    ½ cup dandelion roots

Procedure:
    Boil for 20 minutes in an enamel pot. Leave overnight and drain the next morning.

Remember to tell the plants what you need them for when you leave your tabacco offering. Pray while you pick them. Pray when you prepare them. NEVER sell medicine gathered this way.

MINNIGAAN (skin salve)
Use for diabetes ulcers. This medicine draws infections out and allows wounds to heal. It is also great for insect bites or pinch blisters. I've even used it for sore throats. If you have a muscle ache, rub some in and apply warm clothes.

Ingredients:
    spruce gum
    bear fat (vegetable Crisco can be substituted)
    red willow bark
    black poplar tar
Note: The black poplar component of Minnigaan is only available for harvesting for about two weeks in the spring.

Dosage:
    Apply directly to wound or use a cheesecloth to apply Minnigaan to infected area overnight.

From the forest, some natural healers and their properties

- red willow bark (boiled) —contains natural aspirin
- dandelion root—lowers cholesterol
- burdock root—helps cleanse the blood
- juniper—breaks up kidney stones and cleanses the kdneys
- black birch—cleanses blood; eases back strain
- mountain ash—soothes arthritis, lumbago, and gout
- yellow birch—helps heal damaged back discs and cleanses spleen
- tamarack—helps urinary tract flow.
- white oak—blood thinner for clots; cleanses arteries
- balsam and fir—cleanses cuts; diuretics
- senecca root—prevents seizures

Preparing for the Three Days of Darkness

The following excerpt is quoted by permission of Byron Kirkwood, author of *Survival Guide for the New Millennium* (Blue Dolphin Publishing).

This is a critical time that must be prepared for separately. It is predicted that there will be three or more days of darkness at the time of the planets turning. (Also, due to unprecedented volcanic eruptions. Authors' note.) During the turning the gravitational field will be out of whack. The wave of energy that contributes to the polar shift may cause our electronic devices not to work for a while. If these predictions are accurate, something as simple as a flashlight might not work.

My suggestion is to prepare to handle several critical areas. One: you will need some form of light to handle emergencies, instill comfort in yourself and others, disseminate meals, etc. I suggest that you have flashlights handy within easy reach. But they might not work during some or all of this period. So, I would also have a supply of candles, kerosene lamps, and/or 'break lights'. I suggest chemical lights be used as the main source of light. They don't consume the oxygen in the room or contain any form of flame that might start a fire. Candles, when used, should be in containers that block wind from blowing them out. Obviously candles and kerosene lamps require matches or other means of lighting them. Flashlights require good batteries.

Select a safe area and seal off this room or area you plan on using during this period. This means seal windows and cracks beneath doors so that the contaminated air will not enter the room. However, you must provide some source of clean or filtered air. The last thing you want to do is have everyone die of asphyxiation while sleeping, as might occur if you are using candles and kerosene lamps that use up the oxygen in the room. To seal up the room and yet provide air will mean providing some area(s) that has access to the outside air with filters installed. An ideal place to install a filtered air inlet would be where there is a good supply of unfiltered air available but where this space is protected from the outside of the building. Thus the filter might be installed in the floor where the house or shelter has a basement or in the wall to another room that has air flowing through it. This would mean that you need to leave windows open in this other room.

These air vents should have covers available to seal them during the worst part of the crisis, but remove them to get filtered air when needed. It would be prudent to have a secondary supply of air, such as having compressed air stored in divers' tanks. (**See note) These tanks usually hold only an hour or so of air for divers under water, but might be appropriate for a supplemental air supply if breathing gets difficult at times. A diver's regulator would allow you to breathe the air from the tanks without waste.

If you must go out for emergency reasons, or your sealed area is breached, you will need some breathing devices - something similar to a gas mask. The masks used by painters might be adequate. And, I suggest that you have a stock of inexpensive dust masks as a minimum.

Author's note: According to a volcanologist that I spoke to two years ago, a volcanic eruption of any great size would spew out into the atmosphere glassy fragments, pumice, superheated steam and sulphuric acid drops. The combination of these materials, plus the gas (sulphur dioxide) can kill a person in an instant and can rapidly spread around the globe, in less than a month. If there is a succession of eruptions, this could darken the sunlight for many months ... maybe a year or more, thereby reducing the temperature of the earth. One can only guess what it would do to the ozone layer! So, we have to be mindful of a rise in skin cancer and burns. Trying to grow crops under these conditions will prove to be the challenge of a life time! This is why I suggested that we put as much as possible in food storage.

Food and water should already be a part of your overall planning. But, due to the unusual circumstances at this time, you need to have water and ready-to-eat food in your survival room.

The fourth area of preparation concerns the problem of gravity. People could be forced to the floor during this time and the only way to move about will be limited to moving on their bellies. We could experience something similar to the acceleration that astronauts and jet pilots experience. I don't know if this is accurate, or, if it is, how widespread this problem will be. What I suggest in this case is to have chemical 'breaklights' and a supply of emergency food and water near the floor of your protected area.

The gravity problem is probably the most far-out of any of the predictions I've received, but it keeps occurring, so I'm passing it along. I feel that it is better to look stupid and be prepared than to have it happen and not be prepared. One way, you look stupid. The other way, you might be dead! Put in this perspective, looking stupid is not so bad! Besides you're in good company! I suspect that Noah had the same problem. You know who got the last laugh in Noah's day! —Byron Kirkwood

While putting Byron's words down I kept having this thought concerning a filter system. If you don't have a basement, but have a large laundry room this could be used for a "safe" room. The dryer vent makes a good inlet for fresh air. A number of filters can be cut from one large furnace filter and taped to the vent. My sister, while up in Alaska, had to make it to work shortly after a volcano erupted up there. The planes couldn't land or take off because of the ash in the air. She covered the air filter of her van with panty hose!

*Beware of using compressed oxygen. This could be dangerous, especially if candles are used in the room.

Books and Periodicals for Your Reference

Remember Bill Cosby's rendition of "Noah"? Noah was ridiculed by his neighbors for building an ark in his driveway. I'm not recommending that you build an ark. However, if you are in a *permanent place,* you may think about building a solid storage building in your yard or basement. Plans for this can be obtained FREE from the Department of Defense. Please keep in mind that even though these pamphlets deal with "fallout" shelters, they also contain very useful information that possibly has not been covered in the pages of this book. The fallout shelters described are useful in case of tornadoes and hurricanes. They are generally sturdy and easy to put together with a little revision (steel rods?) And could stand up in an earthquake. They are also excellent buildings for storage of supplies if you have a home without a basement, and they can be *locked* with a great degree of safety.

So, write to: Department of Defense
Office of Civil Defense
Superintendent of Documents
Washington, D.C. 20402

ask for—Fallout Protection for Homes with Basements
The Family Fallout Shelter (MP-15)
Clay Masonry Family Fallout Shelters (MP-18)

Canadian Residents: The following books can be ordered from Ottawa and can be of great assistance to you.

86

Eleven Steps to Survival
    Dept. Of National Defense
    Catalog Order # Id. 83-1/4
    The Queen's Printer
    Ottawa, Ontario

Your Emergency Pack
    This can be ordered from your local Office of Emergency Measures, Civil Defense and Welfare, or Provincial Government Offices.

Equipment and information for self-reliance

Earth Changes Report, Matrix Institute
    P.O. Box 336
    Chesterfield, NH 03443-0336
    (call for costs) (603) 363-4916
    This is an excellent monthly newsletter. Also ask them for the *updated and revised* Future Map of North America. This covers Alaska, Canada, the contingent states of USA, Mexico and other Central American countries, and Hawaii. It includes migration areas, pole shift information, and primary safety lands, plus new islands possible off the east and west coasts of the United States.

Lehman's Non-electric Catalog, Lehman's Hardware
    4779 Kidron Road
    P.O. Box 41
    Kidron, Ohio 44636
    ($2.00)

Survival Guide for the New Millennium by Byron Kirkwood
B&A Products
Byron Kirkwood
RR 1, Box 100
Bunch, OK 74931-9705
(call for cost)
Also ask for his current catalog. They carry Break lights, hard hats, dust masks, respirators, goggles, first aid kits, 72 hour emergency kits, long lasting candles, emergency blankets, camping gear, tools, portable water filters, and much more.

United States Army Survival Manual (reprint of The Army Field Manual—To quote the preface, "No one knows survival better than the U.S. Army, so this exceptional field guide is the most authoritative of its kind.")
B&A Products
RR 1, Box 100
Bunch, OK 74931-9705

Mother Earth News
P. O. Box 56302
Boulder, CO 80322-6302
Ask the knowledgeable staff of this periodical for list of available books/articles on building root cellars, greenhouses, putting in your own well, wood stoves, alternative heating equipment, etc.

Medical and Herbal Information

Encyclopedia of Medicinal Plants by Andrew Chevallier (1996)
DK Publishing Inc.
95 Madison Avenue
New York, NY 10016
($39.95)
Or order from your book store: ISBN #0-7894-1067-2
This is a rather expensive book, however it does contain everything you need to know about herbal medicine; how they work and remedies for home use. A very important book. I have it right next to my first aid book.

Alternative Medicine, The Definitive Guide compiled by the Burton Goldberg Group.
Future Medicine Publishing, Inc.
10124 18th Street
Puyallup, WA 98371
(inquire about price)
Or order from your book store. To quote from Deepak Chopra, M.D., "This book is long overdue. Finally, we have an authoritative text which will be a resource to both patients and health care providers. If you are interested in alternative medicine of any kind and want the security of authenticity in this field, you'd better get *Alternative Medicine, the Definitive Guide.*"

This, too, is an expensive book, but well worth every penny!

30 Plants That Can Save Your Life by Douglas Schar
($12.95)

Booklet 27: Growing Medicinal Herbs In as Little as Fifty Square Feet—Uses and Recipes
($6.00)

Order these two companion books from:
Bountiful Gardens
18001 Shafer Ranch Road
Willits, CA 95490
Bill and Betsy Bruneau are wonderful people and will give you all the help you need! They also have seeds and plants grown right there at Bountiful Gardens and they head up Ecology Action. Their seeds and plants are grown without chemical fertilizers and pesticides. They carry fruit, berry and vegetable seeds and plants, as well as herbs. Send for their free catalog.

Last, but not least . . . books on dowsing! It's quite possible that you will have to find water wherever you are. The following books make it easier:

The Divining Hand by Christopher Bird
New Age Press
P. O. Box 1216
Black Mountain, NC 28711
ISBN # 0-87613-090-2

The Dowser's Workbook by Tom Graves
   Sterling Publishing Company
   387 Park Avenue
   New York, NY 10016
   ISBN # 0-8069-7398-6
   A complete step-by-step course in which the beginner can learn this ancient art of dowsing and experience the benefits. Excellent investment.

Again—before writing to the publishing company, try your local bookstore.

Let's Not Forget Those Furry or Feathered Friends Who Love Us Unconditionally

For their sake, take the following steps now or be prepared to do, or store, the following:

- Update all shots and record vaccinations.

- Talk to your vet about how *you* can give your pet shots and then buy all necessary vaccines and needles for storage. Pay close attention to "shelf life" of these items. You can also write for a catalog of vaccine supplies from Doctors Foster and Smith, 22253 Air Park Road, P. O. Box 100, Rhinelander, Wisc. 54501-0100.

- Nail clippers, flea comb, mat splitter and brushes.

- Store, or put in vehicle now, leashes and/or lines for outdoor use. Some cats can do well with a *harness* and leash. Give it a try. Or use portable cages for cats, as well as covered cages for birds and appropriate "travel homes" for other pets. Use anything that can make them less nervous and more comfortable. You're not the only one that feels uneasy . . . believe me!

- Practice making your own dog and cat food so that you need not be dependent on what you can store. You may be doing your pet a favor in the long run. Look for the following book: *Dr. Pitcairn's Complete Guide to Natural Health For Dogs and Cats* published by Rodale Press, 33 E. Minor Street, Emmaus, PA 18098. You may never go back to feeding commercially canned food again. This book sells for $20 and is worth it. There are instructions for making your own insect repellent shampoo. Flea and tick sprays, dips or powder are the worst environmental pollutants you can put on your animals. Ever wonder why these products say "avoid contact with skin"? If it's harmful to *your* skin, how about theirs? As for flea control pills, I'm not going to mention what these do to your pets' liver and kidneys.

The following is reprinted from Dr. Pitcairn's book with permission from Rodale Press:

"Make your own insect repellent shampoo. Add Eucalyptus Oil to natural *shampoo. After thoroughly shampooing and rinsing, try a rinse with one tablespoon white vinegar to one pint warm water. . . . A conditioner that also helps repel fleas and makes the coat shine. Mix together and steep for ten minutes— one teaspoon dried rosemary to one pint water. Cool to body temperature. Pour over your pet. Rub it in. Towel dry. (No need to rinse off.) They'll love you for it and the fleas hate it! . . . Herbal flea powder: Combine one part each of powdered herbs, euca-lyptus, rosemary, fennel, yellow dock, wormwood and rue. Put this in a shaker-top jar and shake well."*

You may have to live in the "outback" for a while and there's no need for fleas and ticks to live on your animals!

Closing Thoughts

I sincerely hope that this book will be of great help to all of you.

I do not see the "end of the world." (Nor does Lisa!) Perhaps, though, the world will be different and we will have to cope in the best way we can.

I *do* see the end of all conflict. The earth will once again see the embrace of the sun. The seeds will awaken and the bees will raid our orchards. We will live as one race— the human race—and a united mankind will forge a new friendship with our Mother Earth and God.

Love, peace and light,
Shirley Jonas and Elisabeth Dietz

About the Authors

ELISABETH (LISA) DIETZ was born in Sault Ste. Marie, Michigan. Her mother was Anishnabe (Chippewa), with family ties in Batchewana, Garden River First Nations, and Sault tribe of Chippewas. She was raised in a family of artists and studied in eastern universities as well as in Europe. Lisa draws on traditional native values and her own gift of second sight for the serene spirituality evident in her artistic creations and writing. Lisa is married to a former Chief of the Batchewana First Nations, Harvey Bell. When not traveling to further the cause of Native rights and culture, Lisa, a Native pipe carrier, returns to northern Michigan . . . her beloved piece of Turtle Island.

Born and raised in Michigan, SHIRLEY JONAS was founder and director of Michigan ESP Research Associates Foundation and has done thirty years of research in the field of the paranormal. Shirley and her late husband Bert raised three children. As a free lance writer, she has traveled extensively in the northern United States and throughout Canada, the Yukon, and Alaska. It is an adventurous life that bears the fruit of wisdom, good old common sense, and belief in the positive. Among those many friends met along the way, she values especially the First People who embody her beliefs. Shirley presently lives and writes in Sault Ste. Marie, Michigan.

Through her painting, Betty, Albert-Lincez or Wabimeguil (White Feather), expresses not only her own growth in spirituality as a Cree woman, but also encourages both Native and non-Native people to experience "the peace."

Other Works by the Authors

Fallen Warrior. Prints from the painting by Elisabeth Dietz and dedicated to the memory of artist Ed Cobiness, feature two wolves with blue and silver colors dominant. Print size approximately 20" x 30" including white border ($39.00).

    order from
    E. Dietz
    P.O. Box 1685
    Sault Ste. Marie, MI 49783

Star of Bethlehem. (Its origin and astrological significance with a delightful fictional account in the first half.) By Elisabeth Dietz ($ 9.95).

    order from E. Dietz (address above)

Ghosts of the Klondike: They Haunt the Frozen North, by Shirley Jonas. Eight tales of the Supernatural on the Trail of '98 ($9.95).

    Order from Lynn Canal Publishing,
    P.O. Box 1898, Skagway, AK 99840
    ISBN # 0-945284-04-7

Prints of cover art available.
    Wabimeguil Art Studio
    Box 1253
    Chapleau, ON P0M 1K0

Survival Guide for the New Millennium

How to Survive the Coming Earth Changes

Byron Kirkwood

ISBN: 0-931892-54-6, 112 pages, paper, $9.95

Byron Kirkwood has compiled a manual to help people prepare for and survive the predicted earth changes. He has gathered hundreds of thoughtful suggestions, lists of supplies and materials, and alternative energy sources—basic items that people should have on hand during disasters and thereafter.

"It was't raining when Noah built the ark! We all should be prepared for many changes in the coming decade. Byron Kirkwood's Survival Guide *is a sure start. A beginner's 'must' for preparedness."* —Dr. Greta Woodrew, author of *On a Slide of Light* and *Memories of Tomorrow*

"Insightful and thorough instructions for those who feel called to prepare for material hardships during these challenging times." —Dr. Chet Snow, author of *Mass Dreams of the Future*

BYRON KIRKWOOD has an MBA from Southern Methodist University and was previously employed in the microcomputer and electronics industries. He and his wife, Annie, now live in northeastern Oklahoma. Together they publish a bimonthly newsletter and operate a mail-order business, marketing products for spiritual advancement and emergency preparedness.

Mary's Message to the World

Annie Kirkwood

320 pp., ISBN: 0-399-14053-0 , cloth, $16.95
ISBN: 0-399-52200-X, paper, $10.00

The earth changes predicted by Mother Mary are occurring all over the world. Now—more than ever—she asks each person to open their hearts to the loving Father within.

"This book has great impact." —Marianne Williamson

Mary's Message of Hope

Annie Kirkwood

ISBN: 0-931892-35-X, 144 pp., paper, $10.95

After *Mary's Message to the World* was published, Mother Mary urged Annie to begin a bi-monthly newsletter to keep in touch with all Her readers. Now, after 30 issues, Annie has collected all the messages given by Mother Mary since April 1992, which include updates to predictions and many new revelations.

"Through these messages many have found the love that She has for all of us. She truly instructs with gentleness, gives us comfort, and above all, fills our hearts with hope." —Annie Kirkwood

ANNIE KIRKWOOD, who refers to herself as "Mary's stenographer," began receiving messages in her mind from Mary, Mother of Jesus, in 1987 and continues to receive messages from Mary and other spiritual guides.

Summer with the Leprechauns

A True Story

Tanis Helliwell

ISBN: 1-57733-001-3, 208 pp.,
12 photos, paper, $13.00

". . . an Irish jewel, far more than a simple 'fairy tale' . . . "

Ten years ago, Tanis Helliwell spent a summer in Ireland and was befriended by a Leprechaun. His urgent message for humanity: "Humans are harming our own environment and theirs."

With charming style and humor, Ms. Helliwell recounts the instructions from the Leprechaun on how humans can interact with elemental beings, as well as revealing the fascinating relationship she developed with this delightful fellow. According to the Leprechaun, members of the elemental race are now seeking to become co-creators with committed human beings. This book introduces humans to the means by which we can meet and work with elementals on an ongoing basis.

TANIS HELLIWELL is an organizational consultant, who, since 1976, has worked to create healthy organizations and to help people develop their personal and professional potential.

A resident of Vancouver, Canada, she also teaches spiritual development and leads people on tours to many of the world's sacred sites.

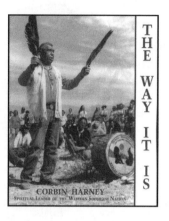

CORBIN HARNEY
Spiritual Leader of the Western Shoshone Nation

The Way It Is
One Water, One Air,
One Mother Earth

Corbin Harney

ISBN: 0-931892-80-5, 232 pages,
105 photos, paper, 7.25 x 9, $16.00

A Western Shoshone medicine man from Nevada, Corbin Harney carries an urgent message for all people to return to a natural way of life. "The Native way," Corbin explains, "is to pray for everything, to take care of everything. Our Mother Earth is very important." He is probably best-known for his tireless work as a worldwide opponent of nuclear testing and as a defender of Native sacred sites and burial grounds.

"Corbin's words are not polished or eloquent; they are simply the truth . . . and come directly from Corbin's heart to the reader."
—Napra ReView

"This book will touch the spirit of anyone who is concerned for the Earth." —Community Endeavor

"Corbin Harney stands as no one else at the moment for that new alliance between indigenous peoples and environmental groups. . . . His voice could be described as the conscience of our planet."
—Stephan Dompke, Director, Society for a Nuclear-Free Future

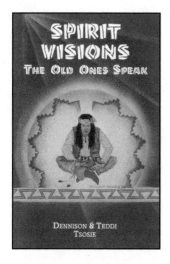

Spirit Visions
The Old Ones Speak

Dennison & Teddi Tsosie

ISBN: 0-57733-002-1, 384 pages, paperback, 6x9, $19.95

This book will change your way of looking at the universe, forever.

Dennison Tsosie did not think he would be a Healer or Shaman—yet that is where his life path has led him. The book, *Spirit Visions,* has a life of its own, and has taken Dennison and Teddi to meet and pray with spiritual leaders in Ecuador, Canada, and Japan.

The information in *Spirit Visions* reads like an Indiana Jones adventure, giving new twists to the legends of the lost Ark and the Holy Grail. His predictions of natural disasters and political upheavals are balanced by visions of new discoveries to help heal our planet and ourselves.

"Spirit Visions, *has allowed me to pull together in a cohesive manner all of the other works of prophecy that I had already read. He is giving these teachings not to frighten us, but to let us understand love and how to survive in the times ahead.*"

—C.L., Benton, KY

DENNISON TSOSIE, a Navajo silversmith and artist, lets the healing energy and words from the ancient ones flow through him. Dennison and his wife, Teddi, live in the White Mountains of Arizona where there is firewood to chop and chores to do.